S. Donaldson



A

# A CRY FROM THE WILD

POETRY BY DAVID LOCKWOOD · PHOTOGRAPHY BY ALAN BINKS

First published in 1989 by
Kenway Publications Limited
POBox 18800 Nairobi Kenya



Design, phototypesetting and colour separations by
Kul Graphics Limited POBox 18095 Funzi Road Nairobi

Printed litho by
Majestic Printing Works Limited POBox 42466 Kijabe Street Nairobi

Binding by
General Printers Limited POBox 18001 Homa Bay Road Nairobi

ISBN 9966-848-08-8

# *Acknowledgements*

First and foremost, my thanks go to Eve for putting up with me for so long, for her love and support. I would also like to express my gratitude to June and Hans Zwager for their kindness and help; Nani Croze for her encouragement; Bob and Posy Zuckerman for whom the first lines were written so many years ago; Shereen Karmali for editing help with the poems; and Kenya for its magnificence and never-ending fascination. The photographer wishes in addition to thank Mr. Nigel Pavitt and Mrs. Wilson, for all their help; and his wife, Mary, for her patience during his many absences on safari.

# *Foreword*

How much longer can life and mankind survive on earth? Why do we need to preserve wildlife? In Africa, how much more natural life can we allow to disappear?

These questions are often brushed aside and only become of universal concern when a mega disaster such as Chernobyl reminds us how slender the thread of life on our planet has become. Our precious water, our precious earth, embracing the whole molecular miracle, is forever under threat. We must keep contact with our instinctive survival mechanisms, which are so often fudged and misdirected within the herd.

In Africa, the cadence of the red-eyed dove unknowingly awakens us. It is there. We know it in the morning, lonely, soulful. The ibis calls and our heads lift, a noisy dawning, a greeting of the day. This awareness of a warm association with our environment releases a chemistry in us which is of essential therapeutic value to our overcrowded existence.

Our anthology covers many facets of Kenya: delicate pieces about the fragile life forms now being eroded, and a montage of raw robust nature, fighting for survival on two fronts — its own and the unnatural mechanical invasion of man. Both Alan Binks and I are pleading here for the protection of the habitats of threatened species.

Here is our fusion of places, people, wildlife and history, poetically presented, evolved from so many journeys and unforgettable experiences in this land called Kenya. As Alan Binks said to me before the outset of this work, "Our common ground is the emotional involvement with our environment".

This book is dedicated to all those who now struggle in the name of conservation.

David Lockwood
"Seascape"
Watamu, 1987

Hunter stalking,
The beating heart aware of life.
An old survival pattern
So near one can touch it.
Something primeval, instinctive,
Every nerve alert.
Survive. Survive. Survive.
And there it is,
A spark of light,

At the end of a million tunnelled
Years of life.
In tune with Adam
And the spirits of early men,
To touch the beginning:
Bone, stone, club, axe,
Spear, rock, bow and gun,
Our heritage and evolution.
And here, as yesteryear,
Walking, running, jumping, climbing,
Crawling, sweating through history
And the last thirty miles.
Sweat drops upon hot rock,
As eye to eye with quarry
Still see the reason why
The hunted and the hunter cry.
The veins throb and heart pounds:
Aware, aware, life, life.
As now as was,
The spirit has survived
Just a glimmer.
As now as was,
That part of us alive
Essential as an eye.
Now scavengers wait
For man to lose this thread.
Then when he we know is dead . . .

Predator Man,
Born small in fang
And claw,
Soar
Above the world
In cunning.
Killer extreme,
Eye fearful
In mind-filled vengeance,
Destroyer beyond reason
Of nature's law,
Earth's most dreadful predator
Revels in an eloquent variety
Of death.
Great mind,
Mindless of destruction,
Ultimate elimination
His greatest goal.
Monstrous mammal man
Struts upon the earth,
Ripping out the bowels
Of his own terrestial sphere.

Cosmic worlds, beware!
Man is in the air,
And will kill your kingdom
"Because it is there".

Rocks that evoke an echo of the past,
and history permeates through to
reach you now.
The unbroken line of time
presents itself, solid and
indestructible.
Miocene, Pliocene and our whole heritage
mixed in this inanimate immortality.
History sounds, the rocks roar,
and time seeps through.
The crunch of stone upon bone,
as man killed his way through
yesterday . . .

Eroded, erode.
There is no future,
after the past and present,
where, at the edge of life,
the over-indulged have trodden,
and sucked out the last breath,
and strangled the life-giving seed.

Unaware, the regiments tramp over
the graveyards of yesterday's fertility.
As the desert devils ride
over the crumbling carcass,
the raped earth sends out its
last gasped signal,
one final aerial exclamation.

The soul of the earth has fled.
The greedy bequeath only
an emptied desert,
and the foetal hopes of tomorrow
wither and decompose
into a desiccated emptiness.

I see the end.
It is the earth end
blowing away in the wind.
It has been foretold.
Yet, still we do not heed
the wisdom
of yesterday's seed.

Morning sighs through the trees.
The mumbling owl echoes edges
Of despair.
Strands of streaked, wisped light
Caress the treeless, long lean hills
And shadowed water.
Rumbling bloodied clouds
Touch the edge of night.
Furred bats flutter back
To dark velvet caverns.
Taloned screams awake
Survival amidst serene
And death-filled morn.
Shrikes shrill and duet,
Chatter and bell.
Voices ring, sound and shout
Territorial battle cry.
The tinkle and mumble of
Awakening day.

Bongo, bongo,
in the night, in the night.
Here. Here.
In the blue-black,
bamboo-knocking,
tree-moaning, knocking night,
I search out the silent sounds
of the forest.
And live through
the silent sounds
of existence.
I live — just.
Do you know me?
Treading silently — silently,
through the leaf-floored forest,
forever alert. A rustle,
and I sound the wind.
A contact . . . nothing.
A man thing, a leopard,
or a bamboo knocking?

Aware and skitter.
Ears, I can hear the footfall,
the bay of the dogs.
The rustle of the leaves
in the valley below
tells me where,
and how far,
it is my life.
I know — I know.
Within the deep bamboo
I live.
Do you know the fear
of the crackle of a leaf?
The unnatural footfall
that distorts the lullabyed
night — and twilight day?
Stop, listen, and move.
The smell of the predator grips.
Skitter down to windward.
You are there,
I know you are there.
The poachers are in the forest,
into my territory.
Their breath is death.
I can smell it on the
morning mist . . .

I can sense the ever presence.
It is here.
At first light,
the crack of the cut
and the honey'd forest,

my home, is going.
I hear the bay of the dogs.
I hear the tread of the feet.
I hear the sharp, sharp spear,
singing against the grass.
It sings the song
of approaching death.
The thump and thump
of the earth-cutting tool.
I hear you — I hear you.

My doe patters across the leaves;
she shines and shimmers,
graceful, free limbed
and elegant pointed toe,
proudly spiralled horns upswing.
The tipped ivory gleams
in dappled colours.
The sweet scent of her
grass-fed breath
drifts like smoke
in the silver early light.
Dewed eyes weep
for the unborn.
Her withers shiver
with concern.

Now the machines are closing
with acrid fume;
an alien toxic
claws the nostril.
The groan of the trees;
my dear, dear friends.
Regiments of cedar, podocarpus, oak
and small, tender-shooted,
life-giving comrades, lie shattered.
My forest friends are dying,
and now I know so am I.

Here, surrounded,
the last knoll,
the last bamboo thicket,
we retreat, we retreat.
Our domain razed — shredded.
Who will hear us?
Who will hear us?
Only the dormant,
who wait, who wait
for the pesty hominid
to kill off the natural habitat.
And so he will go,
ingesting himself,
and leave the world to
evolve again — *au naturel.*

Follow the rain and thunder.
Pupa bursts
And silken spectrum of colour
Splits into light.
Now . . . instars repeat,
And velvet line flows
Through the forest
in purposeful flight.
Gossamer-spawned membrane
And ovum created in delicate form.
Life's threaded given joy,
Continued line
Of patterned sense,
Coloured, reasoned,
And to what end?
Unending.

Shaded, shade, shading.
Spreading over water hole
With water-light,
And filter-light;
Where splintered light
Flakes to earth,
In silky folds.
And here we see
An elegant tangle
And haven of golds
Tumbled, into branch and vine.

In this serene tranquility,
Where is the fever?
In the water?
Or in the tree?
In days past,
The unknown mystery.

Now as ever,
Now we see,
The patterned greens and browns,
With smooth, peaceful, lazy sweep,
Looking out at the world
With permanent dignity. . .

Spume and spray,
Perpetual motion night and day.
Blue on blue horizons far,
Green and rain
With dark cloud grey,
And spray from shore rock.
The scudding sail,
The wheeling wing,
The timeless motion of everything.
We still look and look
And look,
With hypnotic fascination.
A breaker rolling, tumbling,
Sounding the dream sound . . .
When, sometimes far away inland,
The sigh of the wind through the trees
Some days reminds us
Of the sea sound.
Eternally singing along the shores
Of all the world . . .
Songs of searching dreams.
Songs of peace and balmy days.
Songs of life,
With storm and calm.
Ever to and froing into
A relentless for ever . . .

Hundreds hatch and run
And tumble ungainly to the sea.
Now race against predator gull
To safety,
To water-washed shore and
The jaw of yet another predator.
Then, with all the brothers gone,
There is one who swims alone
And grows and grows
With years and years of wisdom.
Still he knows
The hunter comes.
We, your friends, search for you.
Today your coral effigy stands alone.
Paddling, paddling through the bay
Of your name,
Will you return?
Or has life ended
In a labelled can?

Variegated blood and cream,
Sun-salted, encrusted red,
Coagulated semen of the earth,
Seeping through rift crack,
Mixed and pressed in gunnysack,
Perpetual produce of a mine,
Sacked and tracked to
Mile 49.

Arched . . . Green . . . Sprouting . . .
Crackle tip and counterpoint
With colobus,
Turaco crimson
Flash from cedar.
Antelope delicate, tiptoe, step.
Stop. Listen.
One step, stop,
And timorous into glade.
Jousting bamboos knock
In moaning upward wind:
Swaying in crescendo
With stout-hearted,
Singing hagenia trees.
While the leaves semi-quaver
And eternally drop:
The chorus and woodwind
Symphony plays
On a lichen-curtained stage.
Hyrax conducts, staccato,
The infinite drama,
And rattles the death of day . . .

The womb of the Aberdare Mountain
Bears and spits forth Tana,
While proud clitoral Kenya watches
Over weaning plains and the growth
Of her godchild,
Fed by the breast of Batian, flows
Fat and brown,
Tumbling through turbine,
Down, down, down.

We are the water people,
We are a water world.
Water — the first life-giving form,
the hydrogen oxygen mixture,
The volatile — forever in flux;
with the radiating sun,
synthesizing the life forms,
tuning the matter mass.

Our history goes back only
to the first droplet.
Death is desiccated,
dried and dusty.
Life will recycle
only in a water world.

From it burst Eden,
and Adam was spawned
with the amalgam:
born with the fruits and seeds,
ejaculated into the world.

The singing running rivers
and streams chorus
with the sigh of the seas.
The laughter of the rivulet
before the roar of the fall,
Clouds of water embalming all,
in mixtures, and moving life forms.

The beauty is in a cool cup,
as the swollen tongue of life
receives its fuel for regeneration.
In this circumstance, we know
that water is God.
Dormant without it,
our intelligence would die,
and infinity would be unknown . . .

Out, out of the mists,
out of our beginning
did we run together.
When the mountains thundered
and the ground shook
and rivers ran
red and hot
and waves of earth
trembled like the sea,
we ran,
you two-legged, skinny, hairy
runt,
we ran.
You also ran from me.

The glaciers groaned and groaned.
We retreated.
We retreated together.
Others disappeared.
They died
with my woolly brothers.
We were together at that time,
bred together
in the matrix of terrestial life.
We drank together,
died together,
each alone.
I knew you,
as I smashed my way through
the molten earth-forming ages,
as I tossed away the years
and blistered my way
through history.

I could hear you
and then fear you,
as you called me
with the fluted call.
You lured me
into the pitted fall.

Now bayed
for the last charge,
I am head high
to catch the scent of you,
my tormentor.
You envelop my territory
all around.
The cycle is now complete,
the last link completed
to spiral me into the archaic
unwanted,
the fettered world of the unwanted,
the last vestige of our ancestral
world, thrown out . . .

And now is new.
I am thrown out
like some bankrupt partner.
You liquidate my parts
for pleasure
and for folly,
and leave my carcass
to moulder
in the museum of antiquity.
My epitaph will hang
above a musty glass:
"He was a friend and foe
in a journey long, long ago,
but now he is no more.
He was too big for us."

Your coins collected to save me.
If I could, I would
collect coins
to save you.
You. . . who have lost the way,
our way.

Oh, give me a world
where the setting sun's
a horizon.
Give me a world
to slumber for a year.
Give me a world that once
was mine to thrive on
and lumber on the plain without a fear
Give me a world where
tracks go on forever,
as on and on I circle
in my span.
Give me a world where
I can charge forever
and never ever see
another man . . .

The dangerous myth:
bluffing territorial,
roaring territorial,
a wrinkled, primeval, furrowed
brow sounds,
challenging the successor.
Come,
and stare ferocious,
your silver-backed framed
freedom too complete.
Must we contain it?
Conquer it? Destroy it?
And liberate the world
from all freedom
but ours, ours?

You, whose bipedal body smashes
through the thickest tangle,
searching for the fresh fruit
the berry and the root . . .

You, massive you,
your benign nature
revealed
too late.

Now,
we have taken your challenge
and squeezed you into
the last shrub;
or caught,
caged in concrete,
you are forced to copulate
before the world.
What ignominy to suffer;
captured, you are subjected
to this shame.

Your noble frame will wither
and your family, without its
head, dither into dust.
No longer the new nightly bed
in the green mass.
No longer
the moss-mattressed bough.
You will die in concrete
or by the hoe.
By killing you,
we cannot see or know
that we are killing we.

Hill chat . . . sunbird malachite
In cabbage-headed glabrous leaf,
Roof-gardened, yellow-petalled
Groundsel house.
Beard blowing in cold glacial wind,
Singing duets
With hyrax whistle
And echo
Down valley
Where once the mighty tune of ice
Gouged the rock . . .
Our legions march the steep valleys.
Sentinels head ridge top
And look out into violet,
Zero-temperatured night.
Tall foot twenty groundsels
Command the only door
To hoar and sear-cracked rock.
Centurions stand,
The never-ending, sun-scarred,
Hail-rattled extreme of
Equatorial mile-high
Night and day.

Epitome of majesty,
Ageless elephant might,
Descends the valley.
Free — protected by the father of the realm.
Here, in this valley of his kingdom,
Reigned supreme.
The monarch ruled, revered by all.
His majesty measured only by his protector.
The span is spent,
But what great monument — his legacy?
What great argument his name
Created in the yardstick of our time.
Our time is his — expect no more.
He lived to gracious end.
History's chapter in him well spent,
His dignity supreme.
To run the gamut of our time — and win —
Is victory alone.

Above the vast savannah, Africa
On equator stands,
A legacy of rock and land
Pumped up into the heart of plain
By sunken rift,
An effulge of rock and ice,
A relic
Where no man lives for long
And nature still commands
In regal unadulterate.

Here, birds sit and flit upon
Alien feet
And water crystal tumbles
Through peat and stone.
A forest fortress at its base
Stands guardian and repels inroad.
Queen Sheba knew this place
And Menelik perhaps is rocked
In his eternal cradle.
Facets change in sunlight
And this jewel leads man
To challenge — know himself.

The rattle of buffalo scything
Through bamboo
Reminds the intruder he is not alone.
Warning bark — and black-white -
Maned monkey flies, etching his flight
In wondrous leaps, streaming through
The forest and leaf-scarred purple
Fluorescent lobelia.

Here, on the upward edge of outer Africa,
Elements unending hurl themselves on
Batian's bastion
And gouged, ice-torn, seared rock
Is honed, and becomes a thing of wonder,
Glimpsed through an open veil of cloud.
The mountain slopes — the last unchallenged
Domain of Africa —
Still scream and snort defiance.
And thus it must remain in our time,
In this, one of the last corners —
Let it be.

Cobra coiled tight,
Smiling on the rock of sun-worn life,
Smug, greedy, gorged pupils
Dilate in
Skin-slithered, sin-smoothed
Line of Eve,
Lies bitter-sweet glitter
Around the core of regurgitated
Adam dust — while
Faecied full belly scrapes in
The bowel of existence
And revels in the droppings
From Man's immortal soul?

A night sound
synonymous with death
and spiritual incantation.
The slow cadenzas rise and fall.
Hyenas
call, in the black, dark,
whooping, eerie, renting
nightness.
Ghouls rise from the dead
and flee at the sound
of the coming devil's undertaker.
Hear the giggle and cackle,
as the massive-jawed witches
guard the festering cadaver,
as they slaver in the bowel
of death,
and niggle and squabble
over the unfortunate.
It is a call
evil in the blackness.
The hunter knows
it is death.
Where is death?
It is a call we heard
from the cave.
A song, from the beginning.
"Come, brothers!
Together we are strong
and hunt tonight."
Or each alone
sniff out the dying.
Tomorrow, an odd bone
will witness a passing
of the spirit freed,
and Africa gleaned
of yesterday's carnage.
Now, the marshalling, limping,
hyena
will forever feed
while life breathes its last
on the plain . . .

Rapier eye feared,
Roar and cavernous reeking maw,
Rippled majesty in the gore of
Yesterday's kill.
Fear-pregnant night — relentless
Path — is his domain.
Pastured flesh, sleek and fat, provide
The larder of his land
And know inevitable end.
Foxy friends follow in his wake
And time will come when
The lord has fed.
Despotic king, who rules by strength,
Great power,
And he, like all, reigns for an hour
Then in his turn will fall,
Lie perished — strength devoured —
Digested by ant and worm.
And progeny prowl in father's pad.
Remember — Remember days of
Conquest and glory — But today,
Today at any price — survive —
For man's device?

Undulating,
Yellow fever weavering,
Wandering, over hill
And flint bao board,
Rocks tumble and crack.
Games played, times,
Since games began,
And elegant antelope ran
In unending competition with clock.
Carved rock, arrow design,
And still hills undulate
And time,
Stands unchanged for them.

Descend into depression,
Ash-grey, tinged-pink lake,
Rudely regimented urban me,
Into the bowl of timeless Africa.
Down — down out of the time see
Masticated morsel of other dimension,
Ruminated rhythm of infinite repetition.
Ascend into time —
And confirmed relativity.

Proboscis probing for the saline earth,
Knees bend and ivory digs.
The satanic sensations of the forest night
Gives me and mine an intruder's feeling.
Permanent moonlight invades the privacy
Of Africa nocturnal.
*Panthera* pads,
The night becomes alive.
While Africa sleeps,
It also wakes.

Gnarled . . . creased . . . tusked . . . whisked
Snouting . . . kneeling . . . rooting,
Erect tail speeding,
Swishing through grassy plain,
Family scampers aft.
Piglets puddle and squeal,
Sow contented grunts,
Snuggle and suckle on blissful nipple.

Plains flecked . . . gold, cloaked in
Fused last lights,
Sink down into soft sleepy night
And rough, earthy, skin-crinkled heaven.

Camel bells — camel bells.
Here, among the wells of life-giving wate
And parched, flecked, fly-blown carcass,
We understand the beauty of life —
Torn, blistered retinas gaze
From the sanctuary of the wet sand patch
To the soaring wings, who claw life out
Of death.
God is good.
Allah be praised.
With cracked lips upon our knees,
In unison with all creeds,
We suck life from the sand
And the ringing wooden clack,
A joyous sound.

Gerenuk nibble bush top sweet.
Dikdik scamper beneath the feet
of whistling thorn.
Proud Samburu prance and preen.
Shapes slide beneath malingering
water, dark, unseen.
Carnivores crunch on kill
and rumble low,
bounding their territorial . . .

Squared miles of red-funnelled,
Termite-hilled Africa;
Bark of shattered baobab,
Shredded by starved herds;
Tuskers splashed red in sunset;
Mothers and herds scream
At unjust sun;
Sapless black stumps jut to horizon
In timeless jigsaw of survival.
The weak are flayed
And crumple one by one,
And vultures flight
To bloat upon the drought,
Until shoots grow green
And winged beaks
Glide
Into times lean.

There was a time
when the dawn revealed
the mammoth shapes
moving quiet:
sponging, tyre-tread tracking,
matriarch-demanding, loving,
coddling,
with space and time,
heaving across the vast savannah,
trekking to water,
to water.
Through copse, glade, forest;
Seed-eating, sansevieria-chewing,
tree-crashing and crunching;
the trunked hands weaving, splashing,
drawing the water,
tearing the tuft,
sounding the wind.
The flapping great ears
cooling the blood
under the shaded *tortilis,*
in the sizzling, fly-buzzing,
equatorial, mirage-wavering,
stifling noon.
Bellys' rumble and grumble,
talking,
a whispered, trembling communication . . .

Our perennial wandering
to the dry river bed,
digging the sanded bank,
filling the boiling belly tank.
Now, at the water-holes,
man waits for us.
We smell the water
and the danger.
Our choice?
Drink and die . . .

The rain-sound chatter
of the man machine,
the searing metal thorns
tearing
the babies, the mothers, the
aunties all,
and our great father falls
under the onslaught.
His proud ivory lashes the sky
and sinks down,
a dust-flying, earth-shattering,
loud, whimpering crash,
and a shuddering last exhalation.

Our undoing is twofold.
The ivory we carry is the
price of our pain,
and our intelligence
a challenge to man.
Now we flee, we have no dignity
or order;
with the matriarchs gone
how can we know the way?
The garrotting, gunning, spear-gouging,
running man
now rules our day.

Once we walked together on the land.
Once we ran together,
when the powdered-singed plains
puffed in the unremitting sun.
Now they have stolen our water,
now they have stolen our land.
Now they have conquered my kingdom
and kill us out of hand.

The remnants of my desultory clan
stagger here and there,
limited by the sparking wire.
And in the vast open desert spaces
I look out for trunk and tusk
and see not one.
Just the sun, me and memory.

Tombs of crumbled coral
lead on to arched doors.
Sunken courts and conduits,
long since dried, fed once
the bidets and flowed with the
chatter of ladies
in closed gardens.
Bowls of fine Cathay
set in crinkled walls,
wells drawn . . .
to wash the shuffle feet,
then Allah worship
in the great mosque.
Into the palace,
where white-robed,
silver-dagger-decked
men of substance
strode and ruled superior.
With monsoon flowed silk rugs
and jugs of other worlds.
Walled green palm and baobab
echo sounds of Mecca.
Now the wind mourns
the dead city,
between arched rock
and tall, timeless trees
and tourist fees,
to succour crumbling walls
and a strangled heritage.

And now, in this time,
go in peace from these walls.
Go with a quiet heart
and refined spirit.
Go with the knowledge
that many have gone before
with grace and confidence.
Go with the understanding
that history humbles us
in the light,
that sophistication
is not of our making.
And, in the millennia to come,
men will sit upon
your walls of history
and, *inshallah,* will say,
"They walked with grace".

*Lala salaama.*

The rattle of a million hearts still beating,
Forgotten and yet ascending in time
With jangle of chain behind.
Rhythm of life unending,
Transcend through the magic of a tree
Bone-beaten, staccato story.
Whittled, hollow log stripped unto
Death
Now sounds full and strong,
Still echoes in the forest and hill.
Your forebears' story untold
As life rings in your trunk
Witness centuries old
A passage.
But cut down . . . sound glorious
With your heirs today . . .
Boom out, bass trunk!
Laugh with stamping, tramping, happy feet
And know your legacy
Will ever be
A sound of joy.

Sea breeze sings from Manda.
Dhows dip and ride,
Mast lean and prow low,
Mangrove pole for tomorrow.
Cavernous street and roofs mate.
Donkeys bray and carry load.
Stately stride and sandle scuff
Those narrow labyrinth streets.
Out of bui-bui liquid eye,
And I languish here with yesterday.
Brave tomorrow — traditions —
And gentle kindliness.

Isolated by the night,
in a crenellated frame,
we look out at Orion's belt
over the minaret,
where the dome of the palace
reflects the light
and imparts the symmetry of life
and all things natural.
The eye is pleased,
and with that pleasure,
the well-being soothes
the troubled spririt
and leads us through the door
of the metaphysical.
And here, we join old Khayyam,
sitting under a palm
under a dome, composed
and dreamily listening to
his own rambling reverie,
which reveals
that peace comes from within
the sanctity of a quiet mind
enclosed in a lulled garden.
Protected:

With the heavens sprayed beyond,
here at the Palace of the Djin
that quiet voice must be protected.

The serenity of shape,
the grace of the arch,
brings security.

The pleasing strength
of the bowed brick
and smooth colonnade
leads us through the many
doors of our imagination,
and with the spirits
of the past,
we walk with history.

Faces come and go beyond
the shadows . . . our journey
is indefinable and yet remembered.
Out of the night a jar calls,
the soft lilting trill
seduces the soul,
then all is quiet.

As we yearn for more,
we know we are seduced:
held captive in the lust
for more sweetness.

The perfume of the night
sprinkles our sensitivity
and captures us in a melody
of sensual awareness . . .
The flower heads nod
and regenerate.
Tomorrow they will colour the day.
But colour is now white-walled,
velvet-caverned purple,
and dark-bloodied black,
as we move toward the
womb of sleep.

The trees stir and rustle,
turning in their slumber,
and remind us like an enormous yawn
that night is for slumber;
and as the stimulus of the day
passes into memory,
the mind, drunk on so much
happening, wavers
on the edge of exhaustion
and savours
the last drop of awareness . . .

*Adansonia digitata,*
Sing for a thousand years
A cantata for Africa.
The mighty monolith here
Extrudes the essence of this
Timeless continent.
Seeded an aeon gone,
Its life continues
On and on.
The longest living African
Stands massive and assured,
Defiant of all the ravages of time,
Its akimbo stance challenging
The droughts, the floods,
And pestilence.

Gnarled grey, lichen-faced,
Elephantine-limbed great spirit,
Your fibrous heart absorbs
The juice of history
And gives out the fruits
Of victory over the centuries.
Our envy rises,
Knowing you have heard
The loud cadenzas of the
Ocean tide —
Since Gedi's glorious days . . .

Searching
For the revelation of yesterday,
Forward into yesterday.
Into our atomic holocaust past,
Did gas intelligent form the universe?
Did a fusion of thought
Create material shape?
After the dust settled,
Was man born an ape?
Or now, we an aquarium
In another sphere,
Our microscopic millionth year
But a second in another eye?
And man, a fart in history?

*Photographer's Notes*

Pages 12—13
These are contemporary Maasai paintings on the side of a water tank near Selengei, in Maasailand, but they immediately reminded me of the old rock paintings in the wilds of Tanzania.

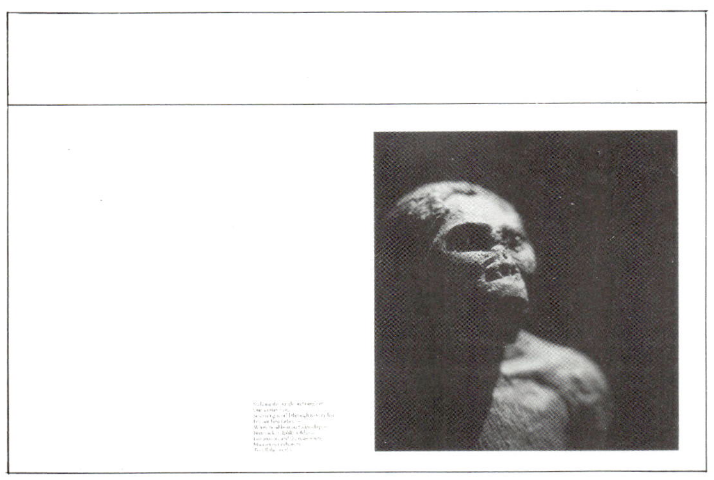

Pages 14—15
Details from a six-inch high clay model of Zainjanthropus made by one of Louis Leakey's students was made more interesting and lifelike by the extreme close-up.

Pages 16—17
The "Gong Rocks" at Moru Kopjes in the Serengeti is a spiritual place for many of us who know it; certainly one of the most beautiful spots in the whole of Africa. When struck with a small rock, the large one rings out like a bell.

Pages 18—19
By including the carcass in the foreground, the feeling of drought, desolation and death is enhanced. (Magadi).

Pages 20—21
Taken on the jetty of the Lake Hotel, Naivasha, this papyrus head immediately identifies this dawn scene as African.

Pages 22—23
Bongoes are extremely shy and hard to photograph. The dappled lighting here is typical of the shadowy world in which they live. (Mt. Kenya).

Pages 24—25
I have spent many, many hours in Kenya's forests and never tire of their beauty. Photography there is difficult because of the low light levels; a tripod is a must and a warming filter combined with a light green filter can liven up the colours on a overcast day.
In this scene, the space created by a fallen tree let in the sunlight.

Pages 26—27
These small butterflies were drinking from the damp sand at the edge of a cattle watering hole in the Rift Valley. I had to lie on my stomach amongst the cow-dung etc., to get the right angle for this shot. (Olorgesailie).

Pages 28—29
Yellow-barked acacias and water are always found together so I thought that by merging them both in a reflection, this association would be visually portrayed. (Serengeti).

Pages 30—31
I spent the afternoon on a rocky coral point at Watamu waiting to catch the tide and lighting just where I wanted it for this picture, and tried to catch that split second when the wave is shattered by the rocks into millions of droplets.

Pages 32—33
Turtle Bay at Watamu used to be famous for the turtles which came there to lay their eggs; today you'd be lucky to see one in a year.
Turtle Rock was named then in praise of the turtle, today it is a monument to its passing.

Pages 34—35
The most spectacular colours of Lake Magadi can only be seen from the air — how the vultures must enjoy them! I used a polarizing filter to cut out surface reflections.

Pages 36—37
I wanted to fill the picture with all kinds and shades of green, shadow and light, so chose a spot where the overhead sunlight was filtered by overhanging branches, giving great variety to the scene. (Aberdares).

Pages 38—39
During the rains the Tana river carries huge quantities of good top-soil down to the sea. This picture conveys the violence and power of eroding water up where the river is still young and active, in the mountains.

Pages 42—43, 44—45
Rhinos are virtually extinct now in Kenya's Parks but only ten years ago one would not only find them a nuisance in the Parks but in most of the un-populated areas of the country too, as evidenced by the skull found here lying on the very top of Ololokwe where its owner probably ended its days cowering from the relentless persuit of poachers.

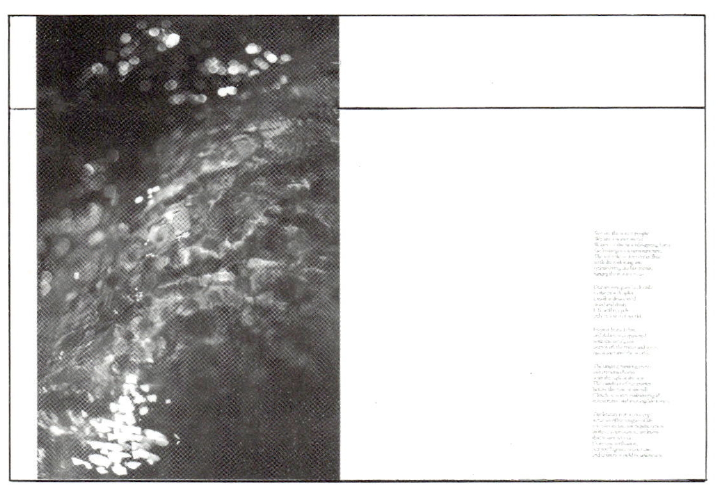

Pages 40—41
I am always fascinated by water — here I got down on my knees in the stream to photograph the water flowing over a rock in extreme close-up, about 10 cms from the front of the lens. (Nguruman).

Pages 46—47
Photographing rare mountain gorillas is full of problems, none of which actually come from these gentle animals themselves. Difficult terrain, thick undergrowth, rain, poor light and a large light-absorbing subject are the main complications one has to deal with. (Virunga).

Pages 48—49
There are few places where groundsel grows in such profusion as here on the sides of this valley on Mt. Kenya. The back-lighting in this view enhanced the hairy look of these specialised mountain plants.

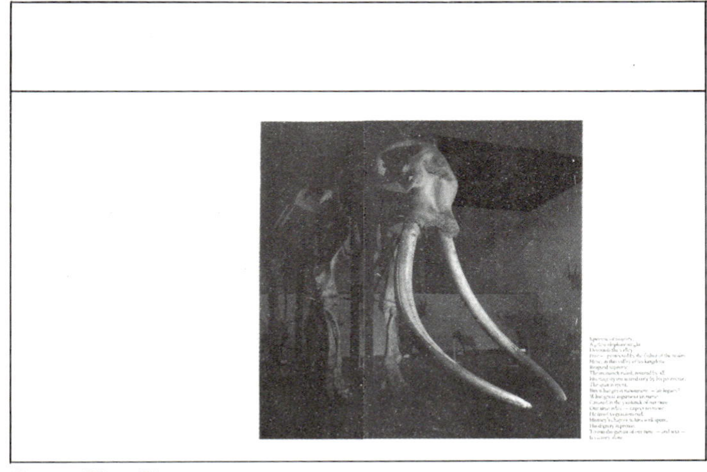

Pages 50—51
I have several pictures of Ahmed alive, being one of the lucky people who remembers him almost as a friend, but I felt his bones might add a bit more impact to this poem. When I first saw this skeleton I was overcome by a great feeling of sadness, like seeing the skeleton of one of one's own family standing there. (Nairobi Museum).

Pages 52—53
The importance of including a foreground object in a landscape picture to give a feeling of space is evident here. What does not appear is the amount of energy expended by the photographer to get the shot!

Pages 54—55
Again down on my stomach to get an intimate view and wearing a snorkelling mask in case the snake spits venom into my eyes, I waved my hat about to make the snake react, pre-focussed on a chosen spot and made an exposure each time the snake passed it. (Malindi).

Pages 56—57
This hyena was waiting for its companions to arrive and help it dispatch an ageing, sick lioness which lay in a pool of water nearby. (Mara).

Pages 58—59
Lions are usually depicted in clean, typically cat-like poses but here we can feel the ferocity and arrogance in his eyes. (Mara).

Pages 60—61

Today it is almost impossible to photograph the Ngongs without some shiny tin roof or other showing up, so I put them in the background to this nice tree.

Pages 62—63

In my opinion truly one of the world's wonders, Ngorongoro is in danger of being ruined by un-caring developers. It is a microcosm of all of East Africa, but too big to include all of it in one picture.

Pages 64—65

The trick here was to try and balance the artificial light from the Ark with the dawn light from Mt. Kenya. Due to the high red content of the tungsten light, this would only work at dawn or dusk when the sun is very low.

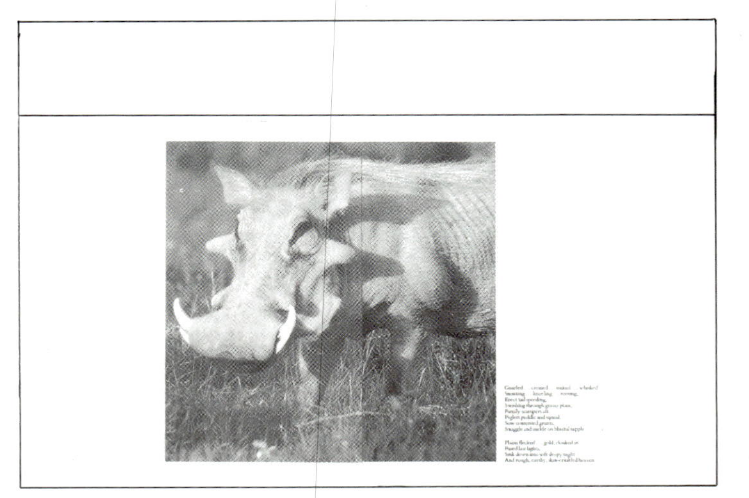

Pages 66—67

Most people who know warthogs well (apart from gardeners and farmers) come to love them for their homely ugliness. (Samburu).

Pages 68—69

Although David's poem talks about water, it is the lack of it that dominates the camel country and I felt this picture had the harsh waterless nature of that Turkana land better.

Pages 70—71

This picture was chosen from many others because, to me, it conveys the essence of Samburu Reserve. Everyone who has been there will remember the dikdiks scampering about beneath the thorn bushes.

Pages 72—73

A reminder of how it can be and will be again when drought sets in. The monochromatic nature of this picture adds to the desolate feeling of Tsavo at its lowest ebb.

Pages 74—75

We chose this picture because it shows the elephant in an isolated state — something this family-loving animal is having to endure more and more these days. (Mara).

Pages 76—77

Gedi ruins are so old they appear to be part of the local geology now — it is hard to distinguish the baobabs from the buildings, the moss-covered walls from the trees.

Pages 78—79

Rather than a picture of a drum, I thought this picture of a tree killed to make a drum made a stronger statement in counterpoint to David's poem. (Jilore forest).

Pages 80—81

Lamu has so many faces that we liked the idea of a collage of pictures which fit with the poetry. In fact it could command a whole book in its own right.

Pages 82—83

Although not strictly a conservation-oriented subject for this book, this place has been the crucible for so much of what David has written we felt it had to be included. (Djin Palace).

Pages 84—85
Some of the Baobabs at Kilifi are the oldest on the Kenya coast. One estimates their age by allowing 100 years for each 5 feet of girth.

Pages 86—87
Actually the surface of a fast-moving stream, this picture to me resembles the depths of space with some ill-defined gas-like clouds behind the stars.